This edition published by Ravette Publishing 2006.

Printed and bound in Belgium

ISBN 10: 1-84161-257-X
ISBN 13: 978-1-84161-257-7

RR
RAVETTE PUBLISHING

All men are
created
equal
...equally
useless

Any woman is going to go out of her mind when she looks at her husband one day and realises

that she is not living with a man any longer. She is living with a reclining chair that burps.

Dad's
in the
garden!

When I said
'I do'...
I didn't mean
everything

Sometimes I wake up

grumpy,

and sometimes

I let him sleep

a little
more
action

If at first you don't succeed,

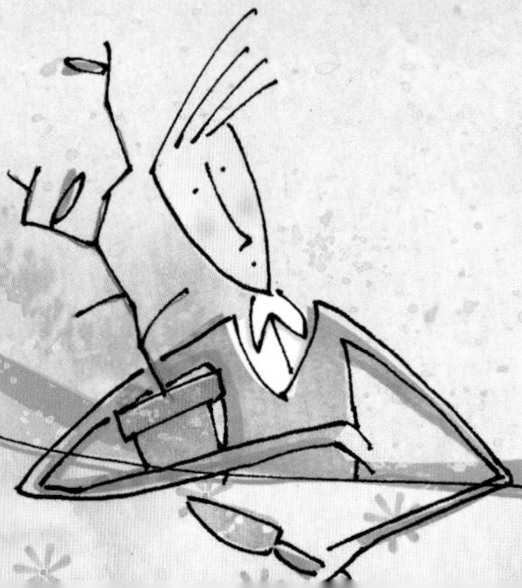

try it your
wife's
way

Three things real men can't say ...

THIS WAY THAT WAY LOST

I'm wrong,
I'm lost, I
can't fix
it

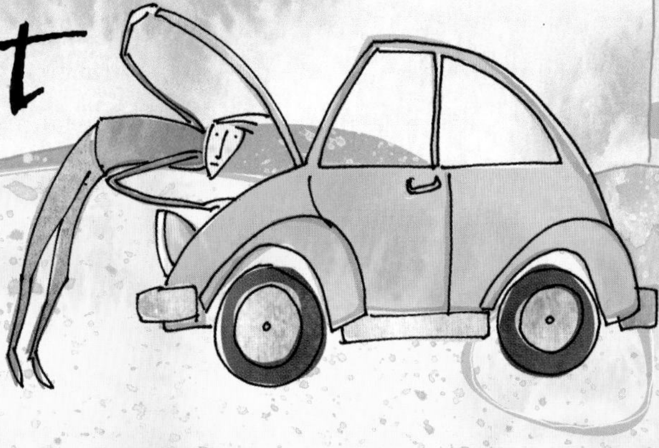

A real man
can barbie
any time,
anywhere

I want a man
who's kind
and understanding.

I can only please one person per day.

Today is not your day.

Whatever women do they must do twice as well as men to be half as good.

When I married Mr. Right

I didn't know
his first
name was
always

You have to
kiss a lot
of frogs to
find a prince

Kids get colds,
men get flu,
women get
on with it

Would you like to speak to the man in charge or the woman who knows what's happening?

We may not
have it all together
but together we
have it all